BORA BORA

© Copyright by les éditions du Pacifique 1974 — 1980
10, ave Bruat Papeete — Tahiti
Typeset in France by Publications Elysées
printed in Japan by Shumposha Photo Printing

ISBN: 2.85700-016.2

BORA BORA

photography   Erwin Christian

text   Erwin Christian   Raymond Bagnis

les éditions du pacifique.

summary

the beginning

A thousand and more years before Colombus, when European seafarers dared not lose sight of land, a tall athletic people were already braving the largest Ocean on this earth. Sailing for generations from island to island towards the rising sun, these long-distance mariners acquired a unique knowledge of ship-building and navigation. Their large sennit-bound double canoes could easily accomodate the men, their women and children, the live stock and plants, as they migrated to form the nucleus of a new settlement. The Society Islands with their mild temperate climate, their high mountains and deep lush valleys, their rivers and creeks, their barrier reef protected lagoons teeming with fish, were most hospitable to the Polynesians. The inhabitants of these islands developed their own culture, arts and crafts, social and religious customs; and yet an echo of the west from where they had come. All history was passed from generation to generation through songs and chants which recounted their myths, their fabulous voyages and adventures.

Taaroa (the unique one) was the beginning of all things. He was his own parent having no father or mother. He was a myriad things at the same time, and gave himself his name. For eons of time he sat in a self-made shell floating in endless space. At last he broke his shell, and called out into the emptiness. There was no reply. He made another shell, and retired for another untold period. Once more he broke out of the shell which became the foundation of the world while the other shell became the dome of the sky. Eventually he created Havai'i (Raiatea) "invoked space that filled" and the first gods.

Other islands were born in similar fashion; and after the land was created it was filled with trees, plants, insects and animals, and the ocean was filled with fish. The gods had their sacred dwellings but the land was meant for man. So Taaroa conjured up Ti'i, the very first man in this world. Ti'i took as wife the goddess Hina, and their children became the royalty. When Ti'i and Hina conjured men and women into being these became the common people. When the royal family married common people, their children became the gentry,

4 *(continued page 9)*

and when the royal family married the gentry, their children became the nobility.

But the world was dark and confined because of the arms of a giant octopus who held down the sky. This darkness displeased the gods, and they struggled to relieve the terrible hold of the tentacles, by killing the octopus. But the body of the dead creature was still obscuring the light, and darkness continued to envelop the earth. Now the demi-gods were born, amongst them Maui and his brothers, and Ru, the navigator. The darkness bothered them, so Ru tried to lief up the sky. He succeeded in raising it a little, but became hunchbacked, and ruptured himself so badly that his intestines floated away to settle forever as clouds above the mountains of Bora Bora where they are called *Rua nu'u a Ru* (source of hosts of Ru). Finally, the clever Maui with the help of the god Tane propped up the sky and cut away the tentacles with shells. The detached arms of the octopus fell to the south, and became the Austral Islands. For the first time the people saw light, and they could look at clouds in the sky. But when night came there was still confusion. This was the time when the first place of worship was erected at Opoa in Havai'i (Raiatea). It was dedicated to Taaroa, and Maui was the first priest. Seeing the confusion, Maui asked the powerful gods for help, and they brought order into the world. They assigned orbits to the planets, and gave the stars their paths. They created more animals for man for food, and trees from which to build ships. The different functions of the lesser gods was decided, and the winds were told their directions. Thus Pere from Bora Bora settled in the volcano Kilauea on the island of Hawaii, becoming Pele the goddess of fire, and Rapatia, the West Wind from Bora Bora became the wind of destruction. At last fire was also obtained by man; and when Maui noosed the sun, and obliged it to move slowly across the sky, everybody in this world was pleased.

the marae

The ancient *marae* were grounds reserved for ceremonies mainly of a religious nature. It was also there that everything of importance took place: inauguration of a king, marriage, council of war, celebration of a victory, treaties of peace, preparation for a voyage, and, of course, to ask favors of the gods. When laying the foundation stone for an important *marae,* a human sacrifice was required to consecrate the site. The principal feature of a *marae* was the *ahu,* a platform of upright stones, usually situated at the end of a rectangular enclosure, where family members and bodies of important enemies slain in battle, were buried. Most *marae* were ancestral and belonged to a certain family or clan. Accordingly, the size of a *marae* would depend on the importance and influence of the family, which often extended over the entire island and even island groups. Women were never permitted inside the *marae* court-unless the ruler happened to be a female. In Bora Bora over forty of these open air temples have been identified. Unlike the *marae* of Tahiti, which were built mainly of volcanic stones, the *ahu* of the Bora Bora *marae* were constructed of coral slabs, some of them ten feet high.

The first royal *marae* of Bora Bora was Vaiotaha (water of the man of war bird), where the earliest rulers of the island were invested with the most important of all the royal insignia, the *marotea,* or yellow girdle, in contrast to the *marorua,* or red girdle, worn by the kings of Raiatea. Very skillfully worked from fine strong threads of bark, banyan cloth and yellow *ura* feathers, closely set to imitate a bird's plumage, the *marotea* was ornamented on its edge with red *ura* feathers and tipped with black feathers of the Man-of-war bird. The stitching was done with a long polished needle of human bone which was never taken out of the garment. For each successive monarch a new fold was added: a sacred performance which was complete only when a human victim was sacrificed. The *marotea* was 18 feet long and one foot wide. In later times the kings of Bora Bora were given the royal girdle in ceremonies performed at *marae* Farerua (double house). Almost no stones remain on Vaiotaha, which was situated in the Nunue district. For prestige, identification and heritage, stones from the most ancient *marae* were often used as cornerstones of new ones.

On the island of Bora Bora there is a large stone shaped like a turtle. This turtle stone, *ofai honu,* can be seen on the east bank of Vaiati Brook in Nunue, about half a mile from the ruins of *marae* Vaiotaha. Carved on it are petroglyphs representing turtles and a headdress of a high priest.

In ancient days turtles were believed to be the shadows of the gods of the ocean and considered sacred.

This particular stone is of rare importance because it was considered the parent of the Island of Bora Bora, and therefore the ancestor of the royal family. From the mating of the turtle stone with Hohorai, the cliff of Mount Pahia, Firiamata o Vavau, the first chief of Bora Bora, was born. At his birth, Vavau became the first name for the Island.

13

legends of hiro

Hiro, the god of thieves, was known for his fabulous exploits throughout Polynesia. His talisman was the dragonfly, used by thieves at night to blind the victims they robbed.

On Bora Bora, Hiro had his hideout on the southern tip of Toopua Island. Deciding to steal it one night, he had already detached a large chunk of land and was towing it away, when his fetish cock, and ever-present companion, started to crow. This made Hiro lose his miraculous power since his magic worked only between sunset and the first cockcrow. Furious, Hiro hit the cock so violently that the bird was hurled against the face of Mount Pahia, where its imprint is still visible today. Thwarted, poor Hiro abandoned his sinking double canoe and fled.

Since then, the land Hiro tried to steal is called the islet of Toopua-iti, and submerged between it and Toopua Island parallel rocks are known as Hiro's Canoe.

Deep in Toopua is a magnificent rock which when struck rings like a bell—of course, Hiro's Bell.

Nearby, Hiro and his son Marama used to play *timoraa,* a Polynesian game of skill with stones. It required the players to take a stone from a heap, toss it in the air with one hand, retrieve it in a coconut husk held in the other, and deposit the stone. The player who thus tossed and retrieved all of his stones, first and without missing, was the winner. Well, one time the two giants were playing *timoraa,* having fun and tossing about huge rocks. Just when the faster Marama was about to pick up his last stone, Hiro kicked it away making Marama stumble and miss. The enraged Marama refused to play again with his father and the enormous stones remained there to this day where they are called *timoraa o Hiro.*

Ru, the navigator, who partially raised the sky, named and co-ordinated the cardinal points before embarking on a long voyage with his sister Hina. They returned much later from Te ao tea roa (New Zealand) in their canoe Te apori (the hull), their voyage immortalised in a chant:

"O Ru, what land is this rising upon
[the horizon?
"It is Porapora, let its watchword be,
"Porapora the great, the first born,
"Porapora with the fleet that strikes
[both ways.
"Porapora of the silent, muffled
[paddles,
"Porapora of the pink leaf,
"Porapora the destroyer of fleets."

history

Written language did not exist in Polynesia until the arrival of the first Europeans. Therefore, all history was dependant on the memories of the people, and was passed on from generation to generation, particularly by the *oripo* or memory-men and in chants and songs. Each island or group has its own versions, since only too humanly, each island group exaggerated its own importance. In Bora Bora their history said: it was the Turtle Stone *Ofai honu* possessed with godly power who fathered the first great chief of the island and started the royal dynasty. From his union with the cliff of mount Pahia, called Hohorai, a son was born. His name was Firiamata o Vavau, thus also giving the archaic name to this island, Vavau, which means first-born. A great warrior and able navigator, Firiamata o Vavau travelled in his double canoe to many islands, where he had local wives and children by them. In Raiatea, Rarotonga, the Tuamotu Islands and even in New Zealand, royal Polynesian families trace back their ancestry to Vavau. Moeterauri, another king of the Vavau dynasty, sailed his canoes through the Tuamotu Islands to the Marquesas and back. On another occasion, he reached the "islands with smoking mountains in the north", Hawaii. The most legendary figure in the Society Islands, Hiro, though born in Tahaa, was Moeterauri's son.

When a prince from Rotuma in the Tongan Islands by the name of Tefatu landed in Vavau and married the local princess Teura, a great new *marae* was built to commemorate the union of the two royal houses and named Farerua (double house). From then on Faanui, the district where the new *marae* is located, became the center of power. The first king to be invested with the *marotea* on this *marae* was Puni. About the same time, the island became known under its new name Porapora. The warriors of Bora Bora were feared by all the neighbouring islands, which at one time or another, had all waged war with her. Maupiti and Tahaa were occupied most of the time by the conquerors from Bora Bora, and the atolls of Tupai, Maupihaa, Manuae and Motu One were considered her dependencies. The most striking characteristic of the warfare, in which the braves of Bora Bora specialized, was surprise.

The village of Vaitape (left), as it appeared to an artist on the French corvette "Coquille" in 1823.
Hitihiti (above), a young native of Bora Bora, who sailed the Pacific with Cook on his second voyage.

19

They muffled their paddles, and silently staged swifts raids on their neighbours at night.

King Puni was the most victorious of all. His conquests extended over the greater part of the Leeward Islands, where Bora Bora was known as *Porapora i te hoe mamu* (first-born of the silent paddle) and *Porapora i te nuu ta rua* (first-born of the fleet that strikes both ways). Puni reigned about the time of the arrival of the first explorers. He in fact met Captain Cook on two occasions in 1769 an 1777.

Amongst his successors as rulers of Bora Bora were king Tapoa I who also conquered Raiatea, the princes Mai and Tefaaroa who challenged Tapoa I and fought him in battle, and king Tapoa II who for a while was married to Pomare IV, Queen of Tahiti. Their marriage did not last since they lived in Tahiti, and the poor king found at many feasts that he was disrespectfully given the worst part of the pig. Returning to Bora Bora he remarried. Having no children by either marriage he then adopted Pomare's daughter Teriimaevarua by her second marriage, and she became the first Queen of Bora Bora when crowned in 1860, at the age of 19, as Maevarua I.

The last monarch of Bora Bora, Queen Maevarua II reigned from 1873 until 1888 when all of the Leeward Islands were annexed by France.

With the annexation Bora Bora became an integral part of the islands known as French Establishments of Oceania (Etablissements français de l'Océanie). Then in 1957, the colonies became overseas territories and the name was changed to French Polynesia (Polynésie française). Volunteers from Bora Bora fought with distinction in France in World War I, and rallied to join the ranks of General de Gaulle's Free French in World War II. As mentioned elsewhere, during World War II the United States reached an agreement with the Free French Government and established a Naval Base on Bora Bora. It functioned as a staging and refueling base until June 1946.

captain james cook

After he successfully observed the transit of the planet Venus across the sun on June 3rd, 1769, Lieutenant James Cook was ready to leave Matavai Bay in Tahiti, where the "Endeavor" had anchored for three months. But the observation was only the official purpose of Cook's expedition. A secret plan, and the real reason for the voyage, was to look for and find a great continent, thought by some English scientists to exist in the South Seas.

Among Cook's many new friends was a chief and high priest named Tupaia, a native of Raiatea, from which he had fled before invading warriors from Bora Bora. Tupaia's excellent knowledge of this part of the Pacific was very valuable, and he suggested to Cook a visit to the fertile Leeward Islands situated not far to the west, in order to provision his ships with fresh supplies. Tahiti, improverished by recent civil wars, could not provide them. In addition, Cook writes *"The ship's company, what from the constant hard duty they have had at this place and the too free use of women, were in a worse state of health than they were on our first arrival"*, and*"full half of them had got the veneral disease in which situation I thought they would be ill able to stand the cold weather we might expect to the southward at this season of the year, and therefore I resolved to give them a little time to recover while we run to and explored the islands mentioned"*.

The "Endeavor" left Tahiti on july 13th. 1769, reaching Huahine on the 16th, and after a three-day visit sailed for Raiatea. There *"I hoisted the English Jack"*, Cook writes, *"and took possession of these islands and those adjacents, in the name of his Brittanic Majesty"*. These islands, which Cook continued to call by their native names, were, Raiatea, Tahaa, Huahine, Bora Bora, and, when discovered a few days later, Maupiti and Tupai. *"To these six islands I gave the name of the Society Islands because they lie contiguous to each other"*.

captain james cook

Also on Raiatea, Cook met with Puni, king of Bora Bora and ruler of the Leeward Islands since 1760.

Cook did not land on Bora Bora on his first or second voyage, but sailed close to the surrounding reefs and then decided "*to give up our decision of going ashore, especially as it appears to be difficult of access*". Further, he writes, "the island is rendered very remarkable by the high craggy hill, which appears to be almost perpendicular".

It was finally on December 8th 1777 that Cook actually set foot on Bora Bora. Now a Post Captain in the Royal Navy, Cook commanded his third expedition to the Pacific, comprising the refitted "Resolution" and the "Discovery". His first Lieutenant was his old shipmate from the "Endeavor", John Gore, who had already sailed with Captain Wallis on the "Dolphin" when Tahiti and Moorea (but not the other islands in the Society group) were discovered on June 18th, 1767. As Master on the "Resolution", Cook had another very able navigator who later was to become quite famous himself, William Bligh, and a number of other men who had fine careers before them, like the promising young midshipman on the "Discovery", George Vancouver. On this third voyage to the Society Islands, Cook visited Moorea for the first time, and stops were made on Huahine. Tahaa and Raiatea again provided food and water, but Bora Bora was to supply, of all things, some iron. Cook learned that one of the anchors lost in a storm off Tahiti in 1768 by the French explorer Count Louis-Antoine de Bougainville had been retrieved by the Tahitians and sent to Puni in Bora Bora as a present of good-will in hopes of staving off a raid on Tahiti by the tireless old chief. It was for this anchor, now in Puni's possession, that Cook came seeking to recover in trade.

Here is Cook's own account: "*As soon as we were clear of the harbour I steered for BolaBola with a view of procuring from Oppony (Puni) one of the anchors M. Bougainville lost at Otaheite which was afterwards taken up by the natives and sent as present to this chief. Not that we were in want of anchors, but after expending all the hatchets and other iron tools we had to procure refreshments,*

we were obliged to make others out of the iron we had on board to continue the trade; so that what with this and other necessary uses of the ships, great part of it was expended also. This anchor, I thought would supply us with this article if it answered no other purpose. Orea (Reo who governed Raiatea for Puni) and six or eight men took passage with us to BolaBola. At daybreak of the 8th (December 1777) made sail for the harbour which is on the west side of the island and it was 9 o'clock before we sent away a boat to sound the entrance, for I had thoughts of running the ships in and anchoring for a day or two. When the boat returned the master (Bligh of course) who was in her reported that the bottom was good, the depth sufficient and that there was room to turn the ships in the channel. In consequence of the report, we attempted to work the ships in, but the tide as well as the wind being against us I gave up this design of going in with the ships, and took the boats and rowed in for the islands, accompagned by Oreo and his companions. We landed where they directed us and soon after I was introduced to Opoony (Puni) in the midst of a great crowd of people.

As I had no time to loose the first complements were no sooner over, than I asked him for the anchor and produced my presents, consisting of a linnen night gown, a shirt, some gauze handkerchiefs, a looking glass beads and six large axes. At the sight of these last, Oppony absolutely refused to receive my present till I had got the anchor, and ordered three men to go and deliver it to me. With these three men we set out for an island to the laying at the north entrance of the harbour (Motu Tevairoa). The anchor was neither so big nor so perfect as I expected, it had been one of the 700 weight this being the weight marked upon it, the ring with part of the shank and the two palms were wanting. I was no longer at a loss to guess the reason of Oppony refusing my present he doubtless thought it was so much exceeded the value of the anchor, that I should be displeased when I came to see it. Be this as it will I took the anchor as I found it and sent him every article I at first intended, returned on board, hoisted in the boats and then made sail to the north and left the island."

early navigators in the society island

After Cook's ships the next foreign vessels to visit the area were the Spanish frigate "Aguila" under the command of Don Domingo Boenechea. After surveying Tahiti and Moorea in 1772 which he named "Amat" and "Santo Domingo", he returned to Chile early in 1773. Boenechea came back again to Tahiti in November 1774 and deposited two catholic priests in the Tautira district. The "Aguila", which was also accompanied by her storeship "Jupiter", then sailed for the Society Islands, Boenechea renaming them as he went along. Thus Tetiaroa became "Los Tres Hermanos", Huahine "La Hermosa", Raiatea "La Princessa", Maupiti "San Antonio" and Bora Bora became "San Pedro".

Next in the vicinity was the ill-fated "Bounty" commanded by Lieutenant William Bligh in 1789. On April 28th, the famous mutiny took place in the Tonga group, providing one of the great stories of the Pacific. The frigate "Pandora" in search of the mutineers, captured fourteen of them in Tahiti, but continued with no success to look for Fletcher Christian and his mates throughout the Society Islands in May 1791.

Later the same year, Captain George Vancouver made his appearance in these waters.

Just a few months after, in July 1792, William Bligh returned. Now a Post Captain, he commanded the "Providence" and "Assistance" intent on completing his original mission. Obtaining a new load of bread-fruit plants, he sailed by Moorea, Huahine, Raiatea and Bora Bora to Aitutaki; and then on to his ultimate destination, Port Royal, Jamaica, in the West Indies, where he safely delivered his cargo in February 1793.

The reports circulating in London of the people of these islands prompted the formation of the London Missionary Society in 1795, with the intent that something should be done to "convert the heathen souls of the South Sea islanders". The "Duff" was equipped, and sailed to Tahiti in August 1796. The missionary party on board included thirty men, six women and three children. Captain James

Wilson anchored in Matavai Bay in 1797, and the women and children as well as eighteen missionaries left the ship to start the first mission there. The "Duff" left Tahiti, and sailed within sight of Bora Bora on the way to deliver the other missionaries to Tonga and the Marquesas.

Of particular interest was the voyage of the French corvette "Coquille" under Captain Louis Isidore Duperrey in 1823, who spent almost two weeks on Bora Bora making a complete survey and leaving a very accurate chart of the island.

The Russian Captain, Otto Von Kotzebue, now on his second trip to the South Seas, sailed through the Leeward Islands in 1824, and discovered Motu One, a dependency of Bora Bora, which he named Bellinghausen after a previous Russian explorer. Close to this atoll are two others, also former dependencies of Bora Bora, Maupihaa and Manuae, discovered by Captain Samuel Wallis in 1767 and named by him Lord How and Scilly.

The United States frigates "Vincennes" and "Potomac" cruised the area in 1829 and 1832.

Late in 1835, Charles Darwin studied the local barrier reef structure of Bora Bora when on his famous voyage aboard the "Beagle". In fact, Darwin used a diagram of Bora Bora to illustrate his theory of the formation of coral reefs.

French navigator Dumont d'Urville, also on his second voyage to the Pacific, passed through the Society Islands with his corvette "Astrolabe" and "Zélée" in 1838.

Just after the outbreak of World War I, the German cruisers, "Gneisenau" and "Scharnhorst" stopped at Bora Bora before continuing to Tahiti. Their attempts to seize the coal depots of Papeete failed thanks to the vigilance of the local defenders. Later, Count Felix Von Luckner's "Seeadler", a romantic looking square-rigged sailing ship, which actually was a well armed raider, caused considerable confusion amongst allied shipping until she was wrecked on Maupihaa atoll, about 140 miles west of Bora Bora. One of her two 10,5 cm guns can be seen today standing next to the post-office in Papeete.

After World War I, the first yachtsmen started to come to the islands from all over the world. Of these, the French sportsman, Alain Gerbault, made Bora Bora his favorite refuge. An accomplished tennis and soccer player, he introduced these sports in the islands. Alain Gerbault circumnavigated the globe singlehanded in his boats the "Firecrest" and the "Alain Gerbault". He died in Timor in 1941, but according to his wish his remnants were brought back to Bora Bora. His tomb is in Vaitape between the village dock where he kept his boat and the village green where he taught the local boys soccer. There today the game is still played.

french presence

The French Protectorate of Tahiti and Moorea was established in 1843. Lying beyond the northwest, the Leeward Islands, or Iles-sous-le-Vent, had their independance guaranteed in a treaty signed in 1847 between France and England. These islands, though ruled by their native monarchs, were nevertheless strongly influenced by English missionaries who lived in hopes of British ties. In the middle of the 19th century, there was great unrest in the islands and much fighting. In Huahine, Queen Teriitaria, aunt of Pomare IV, was dethroned and succeeded by her nephew Tehururahi in 1854. Fighting in Tahaa and Raiatea came to an end only when Tamatoa V, son of Pomare IV, was made king in 1857. And finally in 1860, when Teriimaevarua, daughter of Pomare IV, was crowned Queen of Bora Bora, all of the Leeward Islands fell under the control of the Pomare family who were favorably disposed towards France.

However, in spite of the entreaties of the Pomare family and their counsellors, France chose to honor the Treaty of 1847 and did not extend her Protectorate beyond Moorea and Tahiti, even though Pomare V willed his kingdom to France upon his death.

It took the arrival of the German ship "Bismarck", with emissaries proposing a "friendly alliance" between Germany and Raiatea and Bora Bora, to prompt England and France to re-examine the Treaty of 1847. France made some concessions to England in the New Hebrides. The Treaty of 1847 was cancelled, and the French governor, Lacascade, proceeded to annex the Leeward Islands in 1888.

Bora Bora officially became a French possession on March 19, 1888. Three years later in Papeete, Prince Hinoi lowered the royal flag of the Pomare family, and June 10, 1891 marked the inception of the French Establishments of Oceania. In 1900 the Austral Islands joined what is today known as French Polynesia, an Overseas Territory of France, so designated in 1957 and confirmed a year later in a referendum.

French Polynesia has at its head a High Commissioner, named by the President of the Republic of France. The Territory benefits from a statute of internal self government within the framework of the French Republic. Executive powers are bestowed on a Government Council composed of eight members, and is presided by the High Commissioner. The seven other members are elected by the Territorial Assembly and name from amongst themselves a Vice-President who has powers over all local matters. Legislative power belongs to a Territorial Assembly composed of 30 elected members of which 6 represent the Leeward Islands. Presently, one of the Territorial Councillors comes from Bora Bora.

The Territory is represented in Paris by two deputies, a senator and a social and economic Councillor. It is divided into five administrative subdivisions, and is composed of 48 communes in full operation. The Commune of Bora Bora with Vaitape as administrative center groups together three associated communes: Nunue, Anau and Faanui.

the 14th of july

The "Storming of the B
tille" perhaps is commemo
ed with less pomp in B
Bora than in Paris, but
celebrations last much
ger in French Polynesia.
not rare for the festivities
the "Fête Nationale" to
on for a month or more.
the 14th of July the tra
tional parade consists of
small naval detachment fr
whatever French Navy shi
visiting Bora Bora at
time, and members of
different athletic and yo
organizations. On the p
gramm are many inter-vill
competitions. Contras
with the modern games
the outrigger canoe races
both men and women, padd
by crews of one, two, or
Most graceful are the ra
of the sailing canoes stead
by their outriggers.

The evenings are devoted to the singing and dancing contest—
tremendously appreciated by the entire population–performers,
supporters, and spectators. Each singing group, consisting of
40 men and women must present a himene tarava (a song of local
theme), a himene popaa (a song of non-local theme), and an ute
(often with falsetto voices, improvised and very funny).

But it is in the dance that the Polynesians are most expressive.
Each dance group presents an aparima (a song accompanied by
graceful gestures while sitting or standing), an otea (a group dance
with a war or fishing theme) danced to the excited beat of wooden
and skarkskin drums, and finally a paoa danced to a fast beat by
the best female dancer of the group, accompanied by several men.
The usual conclusion is either a hivinau (sort of a wild circle of
performers, full of erotic insinuations) or an ori pahu, a slow dance
featuring the star of the group.

For the duration of the festivities the village road is lined with small
"baraques" or booths built in native style where games of chance
can be played, and restaurants, bars, and dance halls are full of
atmosphere and fun.

operation bobcat

With their surprise attack on Pearl Harbour in December 1941, and their subsequent rapid progress through the Philipines to Singapore, the Japanese controlled all routes to Australia and New Zealand, except that across the South Pacific. If the Japanese were to be held, it was imperative that this South Pacific route be protected. From the Panama Canal to Sydney it was a long 7,800 miles. So on Christmas Day of 1941, Admiral King requested the War Plans Division to select a fueling and staging base in the Central Pacific. A few days later, the recommendation came that Bora Bora was for many reasons the best. Bora Bora with its ancient volcanic crater, completely surrounded by a barrier reef, with only the one pass, formed a huge, secure deep harbour for a giant fleet. In addition, the lagoon was ideal for scouting seaplanes. Finally, French Oceania joined the Free French, and with their cooperation a naval base was to be created. Late in January 1942, the first convoy sailed from Charleston, South Carolina in great secrecy. Only on entering the Pacific were all the participants told that BOBCAT was in fact Bora Bora. On arrival the formal agreements were signed aboard the cruiser U.S.S. "Trenton" and the base officially established on February 23rd 1942. Thanks to the tight security measures the Japanese were completely unaware of the new base until, almost unbelievably, the secret was divulged by an un-coded radio message —from the Americans themselves:

CK-181 WASHINGTON D.C. 21 1738 US. GOVT. OFFICER IN CHARGE OF TROOPS BORA BORA—UNTIL APRIL NINETEENTH COMM NINETEENTH FORTY TWO ALL MEMBERS MILITARY SERVICES UNITED STATES ON ACTIVE DUTY AND NOT PROTECTED BY TEN THOUSAND DOLLARS GOVERNMENT INSURANCE MAY APPLY FOR NATIONAL SERVICES LIFE INSURANCE IN ANY AMOUNT FROM ONE TO TEN THOUSAND DOLLARS WITHOUT PHYSICAL EXAMINATION.

Nevertheless operation BOBCAT was a success and no enemy forces came to the island.

Bora Bora has no rivers. Its mountains are not high enough to stop many rain clouds, so water was a major problem. However,

American defenders drill with an anti aircraft gun situated on a hill in Faanui (left).
Still in its original position in Anau, one of the eight 7" guns (above).
The U.S. cruiser "Richmond" enters Bora Bora in February 1942 (next page). Thirty years later, French schoolship "Jeanne d'Arc" anchors in the same spot. The island's airstrip, finished early in 1943, remains virtually unchanged to this day.
(Black and white photos courtesy of U.S. Navy.)

46

in a short period roads, dams for water storage, and distribution lines were built, with camps for the newcomers, hangars, as well as elaborate storage and refueling installations for planes and ships. To defend the anchorage, net tenders closed off Teavanui Pass, and electronic equipment listened for Japanese submarines.

On shore eight 7-inch guns were sited at four strategic locations in the hills. By mid-1942, the island base was servicing on the average four ships a week, and was used in particular as a staging point for many of the smaller Navy ships moving towards the combat area in the Solomons. At peak activity, the Navy had just under 1,500 officers and men, primarily located at Faanui. There even today several Quonset Huts as well as the remains of piers can still be seen. The Army, whose main task was the defence of the base, concentrated in the vicinity of Vaitape, and numbered 4,500 officers and men. Concrete foundations, some used today, and the rehabilitated tennis court are the only reminder of their visit. Obviously the relations between the Bobcats and the local population were excellent. They fished, and feasted together; the islanders entertaining with dances, and the visitors with countless movies—an enormously popular entertainment. Finally, to extend the usefulness of BOBCAT, the U.S. planned to bring in crated fighter aircraft by ship, to assemble them here and to fly them on by island hopping to the front.

Today's airstrip on Motu Mute was completed in fifteen weeks working round the clock in April 1943. For 18 years it was the first and only airfield in French Polynesia, until 1961 when the commercial airport at Faaa on Tahiti was opened. As the war moved on the importance of Bora Bora diminished, and finally in June of 1946 BOBCAT was closed down, and became a part of history. The memories of the American visit remain, and, more tangibly, the offspring, some 60 in number, of the most congenial of the local beauties.

During the years of the American occupation, Mr. Francis Sandford, today's Vice-President of the Government Council was the representative of the French administration on the island.

geography of an island

Bora Bora lies at latitude 16° 30' south and longitude 151° 45' west, and is part of a chain of extinct volcanoes which form the Society Islands. Bora Bora itself must have been born about seven million years ago, and consists primarily of one large island about 6 miles long and 2 ½ miles wide. A central mountain chain runs from north to south along the major axis of this island, the peaks being more craggy than those of the other Society Islands. The principal points are Mt. Otemanu (2,379 feet) and the double-peaked Mt. Pahia (2,165 feet). Separated from the main island by a body of water is the small island of Toopua and the little island of Toopua-iti. These three islands are actually the eroded remnants of crater walls, enclosing between them the deep harbour which was the center of the ancient volcano. Encircling all the islands at a distance of one to two miles from the shore runs a barrier reef. This perfect reef is broken only by the pass leading from the ocean to the lagoon. It is known as Teavanui (the great channel) and is situated in the middle of the western reef to the leeward side and large enough to allow passage for most ships. Just on the inside of the barrier reef, small coral islets have gradually grown as the seas tossed up coral debris, sand and floating vegetation. Some of these atolls are quite long and the most northerly, Motu Mute, accomodates the airstrip of Bora Bora. Another, just south of Teavanui Pass is called Motu Tapu (see picture). A sacred site of old, and reserved for the royal family, today it still stands as Cook saw it two centuries ago, a perfect gem of a South Seas' paradise island. Here, Alfred Murnau, the great silent screen director, using only local actors, filmed his masterpiece "Tabu" in 1930.

Of the many bays the largest are Faanui and Povai, both on the west side. Over the years coral has grown and sand banks built up to such an extent that the most of the lagoon is limited in use to small craft only. Fringing reefs hug the island shore except in the south where Raititi Point and Matira Point have excellent white sand beaches. Much of the island is rocky with very little soil. The coastal flats have a loamy mixture of volcanic debris and coral sand which supports abundant vegetation, especially on the west side of the island. Near sea level, coconut palm, pandanus, kapok, lime,

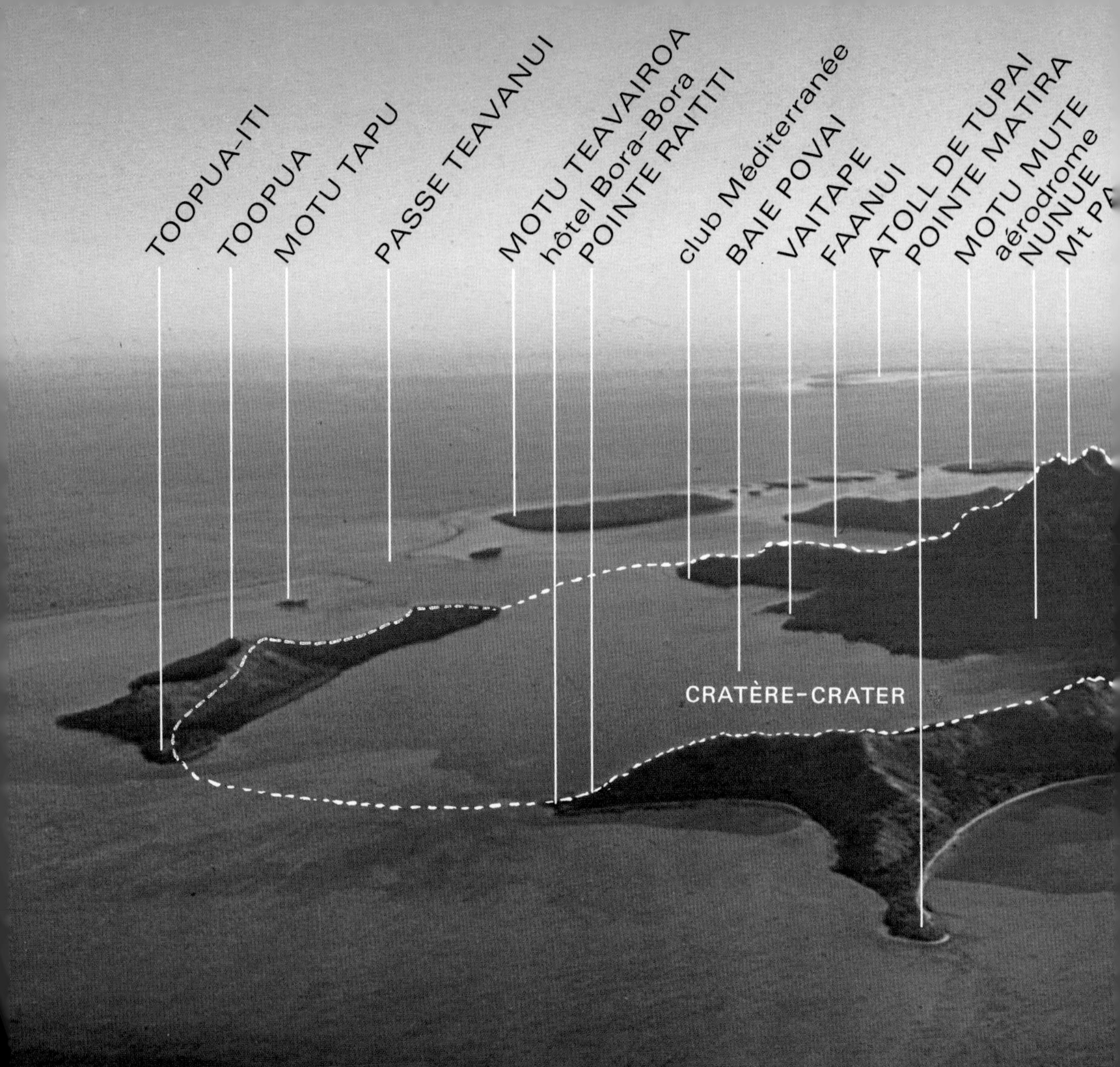

TOOPUA-ITI
TOOPUA
MOTU TAPU
PASSE TEAVANUI
MOTU TEAVAIROA
hôtel Bora-Bora
POINTE RAITITI
club Méditerranée
BAIE POVAÏ
VAITAPE
FAANUI
ATOLL DE TUPAI
POINTE MATIRA
MOTU MUTE
aérodrome
NUNUE
Mt PA

CRATÈRE-CRATER

Distances de (from) **Bora-Bora** à (to) :

Tupai : 20 km au nord-nord-ouest (12 statute miles to the north by west).

Tahaa : 25 km à l'est-sud-est (15 statute miles to the east by south).

Raiatea : 35 km au sud-est (22 statute miles to the south east).

Maupiti : 50 km à l'ouest (32 statute miles to the west).

Huahine : 80 km à l'est-sud-est (50 statute miles to the east by south).

Moorea : 225 km à l'est-sud-est (140 statute miles to the east by south).

Mt OTEMANU

ANAU

PITIUUTAI

récif barrière

BAIE ANAU

MOTU TOFARI

MOTU ROA

geography of an island

banyan, oleander, hibiscus and *tiare tahiti* are plentiful.   On the intermediate slopes grow banana, breadfruit, mango, papaya, grapefruit, ironwood, rosewood and some coffee.

   A few slopes are still devoted to the cultivation of vanilla and manioc.   In the damp grounds at the foot of the hillsides grow several varieties of taro and ferns.   On the coral islets *(motu)* coconut palms as well as pandanus are common, and on some watermelons are grown.   A road of coral rock surface runs for 20 miles around the island, mostly on the level ground near the shore, linking all three villages.   Vaitape, the principal village of Bora Bora and of the district of Nunue is on the shore by the main harbour.   The village and district of Faanui are in the north, and the district and village of Anau in the east of the island.   In the official census of 1977 Bora Bora totalled 2,667 inhabitants.   Bora Bora can truly boast of one of the finest tropical climates.   Day temperatures are never lower than 67° F (July) and seldom higher than 84° F (December).   Nights are slightly cooler.   Most of the average rainfall of 72 inches falls between the months of November and April.   Pleasant winds, the trade winds, blow throughout the year, mainly from the south-east. Sea temperature varies very little and stays around 78° F average.

the daily life

the daily life

School is compulsory [in]
Bora Bora until the age of [?]
and each village has its e[le-]
mentary school. The ed[u-]
cational program includ[es]
recreational activities, a[nd]
indeed dancing, which is ve[ry]
popular. Each school h[as]
its own dance group, a[nd]
there future stars emerge, [to]
continue to pass from ge[ne-]
ration to generation t[he]
folklore of their ancesto[rs.]

Legend tells us that Oro, the god of war, desce
ed to Bora Bora on a rainbow to visit the ro
beauty Vairaumati. The Tongan prince Tej
interrupted his long-range voyage to ma
princess Teura. Pierre Loti's heroine, Rara
was a native of the same island and in rec
times Tarita (right) became world-known w
starring with Marlon Brando in "Mutiny on
Bounty".

Many girls, however, leave the island for Ta
and elsewhere, attracted by the more modern
of life, and its opportunities, much like tr
ancestral sister Pere, the beautiful blonde f
goddess, who liked to travel and eventu
settled in Hawaii.

the daily life

Modern tourism has become an integral part of Bora Bora, attracting many of its inhabitants from their traditional occupations and creating new employment in the growing local administration.

Most families benefit from these activities. However, many islanders cling to their ancient way of life, refusing to submit to the rigid timetable, routine and supervision of the modern world. They continue to live the tropical life provided by the natural bounty of the island. Around their homes roam pigs and chickens. Their gardens burgeon with taro, manioc, and yams, indispensable for the traditional Sunday feast. Fish, breadfruit, and coconut are still basic to the islanders' food, but imported canned goods are popular, though very expensive because of customs, import duties, and the vast distances they must travel before being unloaded from the weekly island schooner from Papeete.

Fishing is significant in the daily life and is practiced in a variety of ways from early childhood to old age. Natives are creative in gathering and weaving pandanus for roofs, as well as in fabricating curios. But the specialty remains the sewing of Polynesia's finest *more* —the Tahitian dance costume—proudly worn by the island's dancers on many an occasion. All love to laugh, sing and dance. One distinguished visitor even says "the real music of the islands is the giggling of the girls". Sitting by the roadside groups of youngsters strum guitars and sing till late at night. The elders gather to sing the *himene,* which are presented during the July Festivities, the major event of the year.

Soccer is the favorite team sport. Loved by young and old is *pétanque,* a typical French lawn bowling game played with metal balls.

Religion plays an important part in the life of the islanders: mainly Protestants, they participate in gathering and religious service often several times a week.

The first missionaries came to Bora Bora in 1807 when Reverend Nott explained the principles of Christianity to an interested crowd. But the new religion was not adopted until the two ruling chiefs, Mai and Tefaaroa, renounced their old beliefs and became Protestant in 1813. Most of the ancient marae and idols were destroyed, the once sacred stones used to construct a jetty in Vaitape. In 1822 Reverend Orsmond opened the first chapel on the island. From Bora Bora this zealous missionary voyaged through the islands—even to the Cooks—seeking converts and making very extensive notes on the customs and folklore of ancient Tahiti.

On Bora Bora there are also congregations of Mormons, Adventists, Sanito and Catholics, all faithful in their attendance at religious services.

Canoe builders, like the ua varai vaa of old, are ftsmen well-respected in a Bora, even if the outrigg-canoe has lost its impor-ce as a means of transpor-on to the wheeled vehicles he around-the-island road. ppliqued bed covers, or ifai, requiring a patient r to six weeks of work, are haps one of the outstand-products of the island. h in multicolored fashion its with its own theme — vers, fruits or leaves.

Once the sole economy of the islands, copra is the dried meat of the coconut. The nuts are gathered, cut in half and arranged facing the sun to dry (above). Extracted from the husk (left) and packed in sacks, copra is taken to Papeete by inter-island schooner to be distilled. Its oil is exported and used in margerine, cosmetics and nitroglycerine. Due to the very low world market price for copra, the Territorial Assembly spends a considerable amount of its budget to subsidize this industry. To many islanders the receipts from copra are their only income, needed to buy trade-store articles of basic necessity.

Many years ago a British sailing vessel was wrecked in the Tuamotu Islands, well to the east of Bora Bora. The crew struggled to Tahiti in a lifeboat, where on landing they were stripped of their few remaining possessions. Upon hearing this, Pomaré I, king of Tahiti, took the sailors under his protection and punished the thieves. Three of the crew chose to settle in Tahiti, forming the first European colony in 1772. The granddaughter of one, a Mr. O'Connor who married Pomaré's cousin, was named Mathilda, after the ship which was wrecked in the Tuamotus two generations before. She married a chief of the Leeward Islands, and together they settled in Bora Bora where part of their property included the beautiful point and sand beach now known as Matira, the local pronunciation of Mathilda.

On this beautiful point the well-known French artist, Jean Masson, lived and painted during the last years of his life. He died in 1973; and following his last wish, his grave in Vaitape was filled with the white sand of Matira Beach.

himaa

The true Tahitian Feast
cooked in an earth oven,
himaa, *a hole dug in
ground to the depth of a fc
and generally about three f
square. A crisscross of m*
and purau *wood is lit c
constantly fed to assure t*
a covering layer of por
*volcanic stones absorbs
maximum heat, all of wh
might take two hours. Wi
judged hot enough, the sto*
*are shuffled about to prov
a smooth surface on wh
the food, wrapped in la*
banana leaves, is placed. *1*
himaa *is then covered w
earth to prevent the escape
heat and natural smoky f
vors. The cooking proc
lasts about two hours, f
enough time for a few r
punches and some singi*
Then the himaa *is cerer
niously opened to the beat
of drums and exclamatio
of the guests. Out co*
*suckling pig, fish, chick
breadfruit* (uru), *Tahitian s
nach* (fafa), *taro, yams, n
nioc, the local pudding* (p
as well as fei, *the wild p
bananas. Your fingers are*
ustensils *and coconut m
the sauce.*

Girls putting final touc
to a tamaraa, *or native fe
(left).*

tourism

Daily planes from Ta[..]
and surrounding islands l[..]
on Bora Bora's coral islet [..]
field, Motu Mute. Passeng[..]
are taken to the main isl[..]
by launch, thus offered a f[..]
introduction to the fabul[..]
colours of the island's lag[..]
and scenery. Built also [..]
Motu Mute is Bora Bora's f[..]
motu hotel the Hotel Mar[..]
(above, right). Beautiful [..]
safe natural harbours m[..]
Bora Bora a welcome st[..]
over for cruising yachts fr[..]
all over the world. On [..]
left the Yacht Club.

The Club Méditerranée (top) and the Hotel Oa Oa (left) are situated in the village of Vaitape. Bungalows Matira on Matira Point (above, left). Bloody Mary's is situated in Nunue (above). Famous film-producer Dino De Laurentii built the Hotel Marara originally to house actors and technicians for his films "Hurricane" and "Sharkboy" (shot in 1976—79 on Bora Bora) and later opened it to the general public (right).

tourism

Built in 1961 on Rai...
Point, the Hotel Bora Bo...

moana adventure tours

The Pacific Ocean waves ever breaking on th reef of Bora Bora keep the water level of the hug lagoon higher than that of the ocean, and crea a strong current out the pass, leaving the water i the lagoon unbelievably clear.

There are so many things to do and see on an under the water of the lagoon that one is best advise to approach Erwin Christian and his able crew Polynesians, as my wife Betty and I did bette than ten years ago.

To us, the best window to the world of the lagoo and its fish and coral is a ride in the glass-botto boat. This is not the prosaic commercial trip, bu one that really gives an insight into the worl beneath the water in Bora Bora. From this trip sailor can begin to read the water for obstruction a swimmer the perils and the pleasures, and th adventurous snorklers and scuba divers a world t be explored.

Once one has found Erwin Christian's Moan Adventure Tours, the only problem is which of th many opportunities to seize and in what orde Christian's boats hold the key to the lagoon be yond the beautiful hotel beach and coral garden

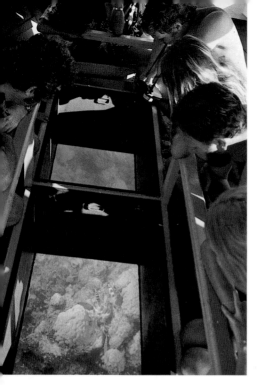

Explore the huge sandy areas with beautiful manta rays, the reefs and coral heads just beneath the water, the deep harbors and deserted islands, the headlands, sometimes a sacred spot adorned with a marae.

Expeditions can include a trip to the reef with a guide. After an intricate journey through coral heads, he will land you on the barrier reef itself and lead you down what seems like a four-lane highway awash in the azure blue Pacific.

Perhaps my favorite trip is to one of the motus, islands which have grown from coconuts and debris washed into the barrier reef. Here on a deserted island one has the reef and its treasures, as well as the sand beaches of the lagoon-side where the only footprint is yours.

I wish I could be this evening sitting with drink in hand, watching a brilliant Pacific sunset and planning with Christian our next morning's adventure in the lagoon at Bora Bora.

Edward McCormick Blair

fishing

The sea has always provided much of the food for the inhabitants of Bora Bora. Fishing, a traditional occupation (and to the native both pratical and great fun) is practiced in many ways. The favor of the gods is no longer considered essential for a good catch, but in ancient times there were gods of fishing and small marae dedicated in their honor.

In shallow parts of the lagoon, *aua ia*—fish traps—are built with coral rock or wire nets to intercept passing fish. The traps also function as live storage for fish caught by other means.

Along the beach one sees the net-throwers tracking the schools of *omaa*—a type of goat fish—where with one skilfull toss an entire school can be caught. Longer nets, once made from hibiscus bark but now of nylon, are used to catch *ature* and *operu*. The art of netting them remains the same; and when a large school is spotted, an entire village may spill into the lagoon to help.

Harpooning is an art mastered by many islanders who can be seen standing on a coral head, or the barrier reef, motionless, harpoon poised, then swift as lightning, transfixing a passing fish.

In the tropical night, lights wink from the barrier reef where *mori-gaz,* or pressure lamps, have replaced the flaming torches of old. Fish attracted by the light are harpooned, and crayfish reveal their hiding places as their eyes glow in the reflected light.

Outside the reef is another world. Trolling there, the catch might be barracuda, wahoo, or one of the different varieties of jacks. They are caught with feather lures or lures made from the shiny skin of certain fish known to the skilled fisherman. In still deeper waters, the *mahimahi,* or dolphin, rise to the bait of flying fish, *marara.* The ever-hungry tuna seem to bite on anything, but bonitos are caught on the traditional barbless hook made of pearl shell.

Today, however, the fisherman enters the world of his prey equipped with those household items of Bora Bora and all Polynesia —the homenade speargun, fins, snorkel, and mask.

On Bora Bora, the sight of returning fisherman in the glow of a Pacific sunset is a daily occurence. Equipped with mask, snorkel and fins, the islanders use a speargun, invented in Tahiti, with deadly accuracy. Very discriminate, they only hunt edible fishes and no more than they need for the day.

Most spectacular is tautai taora, *or stone fishing. It is rarely done, and for good reason, since it requires the active presence of most of the island's inhabitants. Up to one hundred outrigger canoes, two men in each, fan out in a wide arc, but close enough together to drive all fish. The chief signals, and with that the canoes slowly advance with the men in the bows repeatedly beating the water with stones fastened to lines. The stones and the shouts panic the fish, driven by the ever-tightening circle of canoes. On they go towards the beach where the women and children, in water up to their waists, help the men fence in and trap the fish in the shallow water with long nets or barriers of coconut leaves. Oh! to be the guest of honor who is handed a harpoon to catch the fish of his choice!*

In ancient times it was believed that the souls of th[e]
who perished at sea continued to reside within
mahi mahi. The brillant colour changes of the dy[ing]
creature (above) were attributed to the souls' leav[ing]
the fish. Waiting for customers, a fishing boat displ[ays]
its catch. Bonitos (left) are traditionally caught [on]
barbless hooks made of pearl-shell. The catch a[lso]
includes a Yellow-fin Tuna and a mahi mahi.

flowers

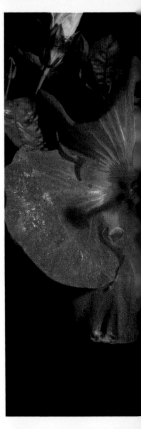

Flowers are planted, tended, worn, and are much part of the life of Bora Bora. Even in Cook's time a dozen perfumes were made from different blossoms. Sometimes planted to define a property line are *ti,* a sacred plant in ancient times widely used around marae, and *aute* (hibiscus), blossoming in reds, pinks, yellows, and whites.

Many-coloured bougainvillea, named for the French explorer, climb the walls of houses, and few gardens lack *tipanie,* the white, yellow, and pink flowers of the Temple Tree. Much in evidence around Bora Bora are *taina,* the white gardenia, *pitate,* jasmin, periwinkle, torch ginger, canna, poinsettia, and the brick-red flamboyant plant.

But best of all, on the sandy grounds near the beaches is French Polynesia's own *tiare tahiti,* well known for its incomparable scent.

The islanders wear the snow-white, star-shaped flowers throughout the year as headdresses, leis, or perhaps just as a bud behind the ear of a young man out for a conquest.

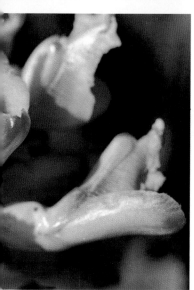

sea shells

In the "Creation Chant" the god Tohu was appointed to paint in beautiful perfect patterns and colours the fishes and shells of the deep. Cone and Terebrae shells were used in ancient times for canoe building and other woodworking. The Golden Cowrie, highly esteemed by collectors, was reserved for high chiefs and priests. Triton shells are still used today as trumpets as they were in ancient rituals. A beautiful underwater sight are the Tridacna Reef Clams. Their mantles, the most gorgeous blues, greens, purples, browns in many shades, are a vivid dash of colour in the underwater world.

Everything serves a purpose, and little is wasted in the sea. The empty molluscs, especially the snail-like gastropods, serve as a home to the Hermit Crab (right). They choose their shell to their required size, and as they grow, they switch to another. Local craftsmen have become most adept in fashioning a multitude of objects using shells, from crowns to belts, from bracelets to bowls, or a beautiful lei, the traditional parting gift in French Polynesia.

A typical selection of Polynesian sea shells and, at the bottom, the highly prized Golden Cowrie.

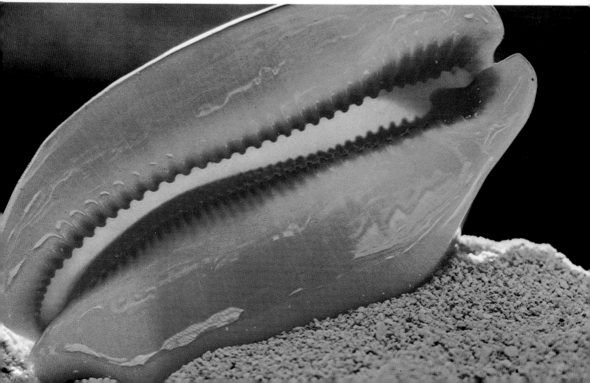

life underwater

Underwater life at Bora Bora is one of the most fascinating in Polynesia, combining as it does the living conditions of a high island and an atoll. The blue depths and pale green shallows of the classic lagoon provide homes, pastures and hunting grounds for millions of underwater creatures, each searching for food, defending territory and escaping from danger. They vary in size from the giant and harmless Manta Ray to the microscopic Plankton on which it feeds.

There are more than three hundred species of fish in this great tropical aquarium; Surgeons, Groupers, Grunts, Wrasses and Mullets—in every shape and colour. Fastest are the Jacks, their rushing torpedo-like attacks sending shoals of silver Needle Fish leaping into the air. A few feet below the surface clouds of electric-blue and green Chromies parade through sunlit coral gardens.

Gaudy Butterfly Fish glide by in pairs. Feeding on the coral itself brilliant blue or green Parrot Fish break and crush it with their powerful jaws. The fragile beauty of Moorish Idols and the rainbow make-up of Angel Fish is contrasted by the eccentric comedians and freaks. A Puffer Fish inflates himself at the first sign of danger into an indignant and prickly balloon; a Flute Fish, seemingly a transparent plastic tube, slips past without any apparent means of propulsion. A Clown Fish looks balefully up from his confortable bed of poisonous tentacles— belonging to a fish eating anemone— (see picture) a deadly situation for any other species and one of the many symbioses of the sea.

Coral cliffs, plunging down into deep water, provide homes for shyer giants and more dangerous predators—for the coral is pitted with crevices and caves. Here in the half light live sleepy-eyed Groupers, sharp-toothed Moray Eels and venomous Lion Fish. Both Sharks and Barracuda patrol the lagoon but are timid in the presence of man. The only true danger is the Stone Fish which lies motionless in shallow flats camouflaged in coral debris. The unwary stepping on its dorsal spine unleaches a very potent poison. Beware!

Nibbling at some grow on the Acropora Coral two Black Butterfly F (left) are never far from e other. So sure is the g painted Lionfish (right) his poisonous spines that does not flee even w approached very closely lying on bluff for its defer the Blue-dotted Puffer (l tom left) has marki resembling spines. Sitt motionless amongst cc branches, a Red-stri Hawkfish (below) waits p ently for a victim. Hover just above their burrows, Threadfin Fish (below rig are quite shy. Swimming whipping motion, this juve Dotted Wrasse will unde several changes in its app rance before reaching m rity (bottom, far right).

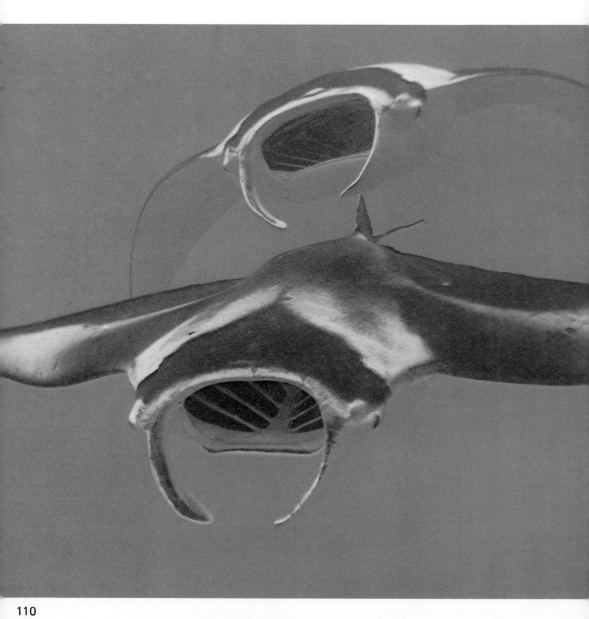

Found inside and outside the barrier reef, the Manta Rays (opposite) are among the largest inhabitants of these waters. Swimming gracefully in a bird-like motion, these rays feed on plankton and small fish which they sweep–with the help of their two fleshy extensions–into their huge mouths. When not feeding, the manta rolls these fins up into horn-like protuberances, earning its second name: Devil-fish.

Travelling in schools, playful Dolphins can sometimes be seen frolicking inside the lagoon, which they enter on the approach of bad weather.

One of the many sea-floor dwellers is the Lugworm. Living in burrows, it feeds by swallowing quantities of sand and digesting whatever edible matter it finds. The filtered sand is then deposited in a neat pile around one entrance (below).

birds

Red, pink, and yellow feathers were reserved for nobility, and from them were made brilliant headdresses and cloaks. Unfortunately, the introduction of firearms doomed the more brilliant birds, and many species became extinct. A grotto high above Anau bears the name of one, *ana opea.* Today, most birds of Bora Bora nest in the vicinity of the inaccessible cliff of Otemanu—the Sea of Birds—the highest mountain.

Of colorful plumage is the *otatare,* or small falcon. His cousin, the Sparrow Hawk— *manu ai moa*— can be seen diving on small chickens. Other land birds are the Pigeon Parakeet, *uupa;* the Golden Plover, *torea*; the Sandpiper, *uriri*; and the Alaska Curlew, *torea,* which passes through in the autumn to winter in the Tuomotu Islands.

The Blue-gray Herons—*otuu*—fish at the water's edge or on the reefs. Very rare today are the White Herons, once considered sacred. Other sea birds are abundant. Called *uaau* are the Masked and Blue-footed Boobies, as well as the Shearwaters. Near the *motu* can best be seen the many Terns—Fairy *(itatae),* Crested *(tara),* Noddy *(oio),* and occasionally the Sooty *(kaveka).* The graceful aerobatics of the Tropic Birds, *maurua, tavae,* and *petea,* are extremely rare, but the stealing other birds' catch Frigate or Man-o-war bird, *otaha,* is a daily sight.

the barrier reef

Millions of years ago, long before human beings existed, the foundations of a great underwater wall were being built around the base of Bora Bora. The island was circular and so was the wall, for Bora Bora was then a newly extinct volcano with barren slopes of lava rising up in a cone to the mouth of a jagged-edged crater some twelve thousand feet above the ocean, looking much as Fuji-yama might look today if it were set down in the middle of the Pacific.

The wall, and all such walls built around volcanic islands, are known as Fringing Reefs. They are constructed by billions and billions of tiny flower-like creatures called Coral Polyps. To protect its fragile body each polyp builds a little limestone cup or "house" around itself and these houses, thousands of them tightly packed together in the form of a honeycomb, are what we know as coral. A coral reef is therefore alive and in order to survive it requires salt water which does not fall below a temperature of 68°F, ocean currents to supply it with oxygen, plankton to feed on and bright sunlight. All these conditions were fulfilled, and still are today, when the first colonies of polyps laid the foundations of the present reef on the lava slopes of the dead volcano. The reef might have remained quite a shallow structure—but for something else.

It is the nature of volcanic islands to sink slowly back into the ocean depths and Bora Bora was no exception. As the great cone of lava began to sink the coral polyps started building upwards, reaching towards the sunlight, for without it they would die. The sinking island, being a cone, became smaller and smaller. The reef, growing steadily upwards, became separated from the island by an ever widening stretch of water. The Fringing Reef had become the Barrier Reef completely surrounding the lagoon except in one place. Here, rainwater carried down from the hills into the lagoon has formed a cloudy current of fresh water and silt which has prevented the coral from growing by depriving it of those two vital elements: salt water and sunlight. The result is the unique natural gateway to the open sea: the Pass of Teavanui.

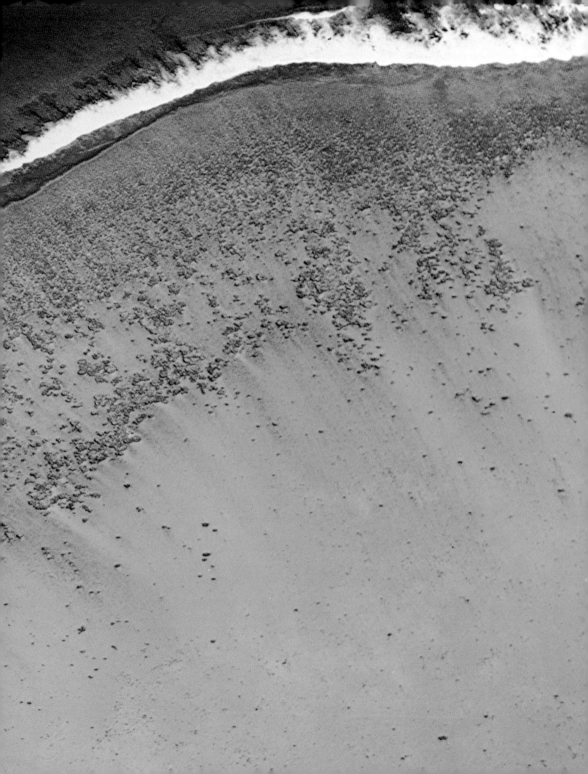

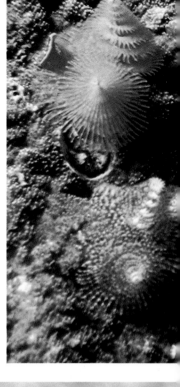

The Stone Fish, nohu, (opposite) is the only true dangerous crea- e of the lagoon and barrier reef. ing in symbiosis with a Sea Ane- ne (right) are several Blue dotted mselfish. Their feathery cilia fully ended to strain plankton (left) are Fanworms. Displaying its en- ged claw, a male Fiddler Crab ttom left) lives in the coastal flats d blocks its hole airtight during coming tides. Gaudily designed, s Reef Crab (bottom) is seldom n during daytime.

colourful inhabitant of the
rier reef, this Blue-spot
Reef Crab (opposite) is
y one of several varieties
nd there. A slate-pencil
chin (top right), holds its
spring   well-protected
ongst the spines. Firmly
chored in coral, several
dacna Reef Clams compete
h Short-spine Urchins for
ce (bottom right). They
d by filtering out plankton
m sea water and on algae
hin their brilliantly colour-
mantles.

By a poetic twist of nature the titanic forces which transformed the molten furnace of a volcanic crater into the limpid waters of a lagoon also produced a race of people whose way of life, temperament and carefree existance has become a legend throughout the world. Cut off from the rest of mankind by thousands of miles of ocean the Polynesians owe more than they possibly know to nature's greatest gift of all: freedom from want. Cold, drought and hunger are unknown to them. They can build their homes and cultivate their earth right down to the water's edge, for keeping away stormy seas and deep-sea predators is the natural breakwater: the great wall of the barrier reef. There, silently, billions of polyps are still building towards the sun.

USEFUL INFORMATIONS

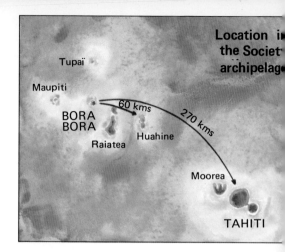

Location in the Society archipelago

Tupaï
Maupiti
BORA BORA
60 kms
270 kms
Raiatea
Huahine
Moorea
TAHITI

Bora Bora lies 270 km north-west of Tahiti. The main island is surrounded by a barrier reef and several islets. There is only one pass that can be used to cross into the lagoon and the airport is built on a *motu*. Bora Bora covers 38 km² and its highest peak is Mount Otemanu (727 m).

population
There are 2,660 inhabitants on the islands. The principal village is Vaitape, with the administrator's residence, the post office, police station, hospital and port.

access
By boat: two ferries leave from Tahiti alternatively every 15 days: the *Temehani* and the *Taporo III*.
By plane: 3 to 5 flights a day from Tahiti, by Air Polynesia. Either 70 minute flight, stopping at Huahine and Raiatea; or 50 minute flight without stopovers.

accommodation
Hotel Bora Bora. Cable address: Borhotel Borabora.
Club Méditerranée, Vaitape. Cable Address: Mediclub Papeete.
Hotel Oa-oa, Vaitape. Family style. Reservations: Tahiti Tours: B.P. 627, Papeete, Tahiti.
Hotel Marara. Owner: Dino de Laurentiis.
Altex Bungalows. 10 bungalows on the lagoon. Reservations: Altex, B.P. 187, Papeete, Tahiti.
Bloody Mary's: 5 bungalows, tahitian style. Nunue, Pofai bay.
Hotel Marina: 45 rooms, Motu Mute.

rent-a-car
Bora Bora Tours Rent-a-Car. (Freddo). Vaitape village.
Otemanu Rent-a-Car. Vaitape.
Bicycles and motorcycles can also be rented. Both agencies organize minibus excursions round the island.

rent-a-boat
Moana Adventure Tours. Owner Erwin Christian can offer you: glass-bottom boat, excursions on the reef, picnic on island, scuba diving.

things to do
The island tour takes you along 32 kms of coral road bes the lagoon. Visit the tomb of French navigator Alain G bault in Vaitape, on the site of an ancient *marae*.
Mountain climbing is possible on Mt. Pahia (661 m). T climb takes 3 hours. Visit Motu-Toopua and Motu-Ta Islands, tour the island by boat (2 to 4 hours) and see Taianapa *marae* near Faanui village (km 26).

CAPTIONS

1—Airport
2—Hotel Marina
3—Bora-Bora Club (condominium)
4—Yacht Club
5—Club Mediterranee Car rental Otemanu
6—Oa Oa Hotel
7—Oa Oa yacht Hotel Restaurant
8—Doctor (J.F. Espiard, M.D.)
9—Bank of Tahiti
10—Protestant church
11—Infirmary
12—Police Station
13—Air Polynesie Main village pier Travel Agency
14—Bank of Indochina and Suez
15—Post office
16—Catholic church
17—Car rental Freddo
18—Bloody Mary's hotel
19—Moana Art Gallery-Boutique Moana Adventure Tours
20—Bora Bora Hotel
21—Public beach Fare Altex
22—Marara Hotel